A Guide for Using

How to Eat Fried Worms

in the Classroom

Based on the novel written by Thomas Rockwell

*This guide written by **Jane Benes Denton, B. S. Ed.***

Teacher Created Materials, Inc.
6421 Industry Way
Westminster, CA 92683
www.teachercreated.com
©1996 Teacher Created Materials, Inc.
Reprinted, 2003
Made in U.S.A.
ISBN 1-55734-816-2

Edited by
Mary Kaye Taggart

Illustrated by
Wendy Chang

Cover Art by
Wendy Chang

Table of Contents

◆ Quiz Time
◆ Hands-on Activity—*Character Profile*
◆ Cooperative Learning—*Poetry*
◆ Curriculum Connection—*Science Research Project (Steps 1 and 2)*
◆ Into Your Life—*Billy and Me*

◆ Quiz Time
◆ Hands-on Activity—*Worm Measurement*
◆ Cooperative Learning—*Worm Terrariums*
◆ Curriculum Connection—*Science Research Project (Step 3)*
◆ Into Your Life—*Sentence Strips*

◆ Quiz Time
◆ Hands-on Activity—*Literal and Figurative Statements*
◆ Cooperative Learning—*Worm Report*
◆ Curriculum Connection—*Science Research Project (Steps 4 and 5)*
◆ Into Your Life—*Wormy Recipes*

◆ Quiz Time
◆ Hands-on Activity—*Playing Tricks*
◆ Cooperative Learning—*Create a Game*
◆ Curriculum Connection—*Science Research Project (Steps 6 and 7)*
◆ Into Your Life—*Worm du Jour*

After the Book *(Post-reading Activities and Resources)*

Introduction

A good book can touch our lives like a good friend. Within its pages are words and characters that can inspire us to achieve our highest goals. We can turn to it for companionship, recreation, comfort, and guidance. It also gives us a cherished story to hold in our hearts forever.

In *Literature Units,* great care has been taken to select books that are sure to become good friends!

Teachers who use this literature unit will find the following features to supplement their own valuable ideas.

- A Sample Lesson Plan
- Pre-reading Activities
- A Biographical Sketch and Picture of the Author
- A Book Summary
- Vocabulary Lists and Suggested Vocabulary Activities
- Journal Activities
- Chapters grouped for study, with each section including

    –quizzes
    –hands-on projects
    –cooperative learning activities
    –cross-curriculum connections
    –extension activities to relate to the reader's own life

- Post-reading Activities
- Book Report Ideas
- A Culminating Activity
- Three Different Options for Unit Tests
- Bibliography
- Answer Key

We are confident this unit will be a valuable addition to your planning and hope that as you use our ideas, your students will increase the circle of "friends" they can have in books!

Sample Lesson Plan

Each of the lessons suggested below can take from one to several days to complete.

Lesson 1

- Introduce and complete some or all of the pre-reading activities. (pages 5 and 6)
- Read "About the Author" with your students. (page 7)
- Make the Worm Journal. (page 12)

Lesson 2

- Complete the activity on page 6.
- Read Chapters 1–9. As you read, place the vocabulary words in the context of the story and discuss their meanings. (page 9)
- Play one of the vocabulary games. (page 10)
- Develop a profile of one of the characters. (page 14)
- Begin the research project. (page 16)
- Write a poem to help a friend eat a worm. (page 15)
- Complete a Venn diagram. (page 17)
- Begin "Daily Journal Activities." (page 11)
- Administer the Section 1 quiz. (page 13)
- Introduce the vocabulary words for Section 2. (page 9) Have the students suggest definitions.

Lesson 3

- Read chapters 10–15. Place the vocabulary words in the context of the story and discuss their meanings.
- Play one of the vocabulary games. (page 10)
- Complete the measuring activity. (page 19)
- Make a worm terrarium, using page 20 as a guide.
- Continue with the research project. (page 21)
- Complete the story clarification activity. (page 22)
- Complete one of the "Daily Journal Activities." (page 11)
- Administer the Section 2 quiz. (page 18)
- Introduce the vocabulary words for Section 3. (page 9) Have the students suggest definitions.

Lesson 4

- Read chapters 16–24. Place the vocabulary words in the context of the story and discuss their meanings.

- Play one of the vocabulary games. (page 10)
- Complete the literal and figurative language activity. (page 24)
- Conduct a worm examination. (page 25)
- Continue with the research project. (page 26)
- Make one or both of the "Wormy Recipes." (page 27)
- Complete one of the "Daily Journal Activities." (page 11)
- Administer the Section 3 quiz. (page 23)
- Introduce vocabulary words for Section 4. (page 9) Have the students suggest definitions.

Lesson 5

- Read chapters 25–41. Place the vocabulary words in the context of the story and discuss their meanings.
- Play one of the vocabulary games. (page 10)
- Do the tricky word activity. (page 29)
- Begin the game activity on page 30. This activity may take several days.
- Complete the research project. (page 32)
- Write a new recipe for eating a worm. (page 33)
- Complete one of the "Daily Journal Activities." (page 11)
- Administer the Section 4 quiz. (page 28)

Lesson 6

- Discuss any questions your students may have about the story. (page 35)
- Assign book reports and assign a presentation day. (page 36)
- Begin working on the culminating activity. (pages 39–42)
- Complete the crossword puzzle for vocabulary practice. (page 37)

Lesson 7

- Administer Unit Tests: 1, 2, and/or 3. (pages 43–45)
- Discuss the test answers and possibilities.
- Discuss the students' enjoyment of the book.
- Provide a list of related reading for your students. (page 46)

Before the Book

Before you begin reading *How to Eat Fried Worms* with your students, do some pre-reading activities to stimulate interest and enhance comprehension. Here are some activities that might work well in your class.

1. Predict what the story might be about by hearing the title.

2. Predict what the story might be about by looking at the cover illustration.

3. Discuss other books by Thomas Rockwell that students may have read or heard about.

4. Answer these questions.

    - Are you interested in

        – children who do unusual things?

        – stories about creepy crawlies?

        – stories about groups of friends?

        – stories which involve dares or
          bets?

    - Would you ever

        – make a bet with a friend?

        – be willing to do something which
          you thought was gross in order to
          win a bet?

        – trick a friend in order to help
          him/her lose a bet?

        – eat a fried worm?

5. Work in groups to devise a survey which asks students if they would do various unusual things, such as eat a live fish, eat a fried worm, eat a live worm, etc. Conduct the survey, asking at least twenty people your questions. Tabulate your results and devise a table, chart, or graph to show your results.

Before the Book *(cont.)*

Before reading *How to Eat Fried Worms*, make a list of your favorite and least favorite foods. Then, on a separate piece of paper, draw examples of your favorite and least favorite meals, using the foods which you listed. When the entire class has finished this assignment combine all of the lists and illustrations into a class book.

Name

My Least Favorite Foods

My Most Favorite Foods

6

About the Author

Thomas Rockwell was born on March 13, 1933, in New Rochelle, New York, to Norman and Mary Rockwell. His father was a very famous artist who often painted pictures of small town life in America. As a child, Thomas Rockwell loved to read.

In 1955, Mr. Rockwell married a woman named Gail Sudler. Mrs. Rockwell is an artist, and she illustrated one of her husband's books. The Rockwells have two children named Barnaby and Abigail.

Even though Mr. Rockwell enjoyed reading as a child, his enthusiasm for literature waned as he grew older. It was not until many years later, when he was reading nursery rhymes to his son, that his interest in literature was again piqued.

Reading these poems interested and excited Mr. Rockwell so much that he began to write his own poems. He then moved on to stories and picture books.

The first book that Mr. Rockwell had published was entitled *Rackety-Bang and Other Verses*. It was published in 1969, and it is the book that Mrs. Rockwell illustrated for her husband. Soon after *Rackety-Bang*, Mr. Rockwell wrote three more books, *Humpf!, Squawwwk!,* and *The Neon Motorcycle*.

It is Mr. Rockwell's fifth book, *How to Eat Fried Worms* (published in 1973), which is the most famous of his works. He has won many awards for this humorous story. These honors include the Mark Twain Award, the Golden Archer Award, the Sequoiah Award, the Nene Award, and honors from the states of California, South Carolina, Indiana, Arizona, Tennessee, and Iowa.

Since the success of *How to Eat Fried Worms,* Mr. Rockwell has continued to write entertaining childrens' books. *The Portmanteau* is a collection of stories, poems, and activities for children. Other stories include *Tin Cans* and *Oatmeal Is Not for Mustaches*. His most recent works, *How to Fight a Girl* and *How to Get Fabulously Rich,* are sequels to *How to Eat Fried Worms*. These focus on the further adventures of Billy Forrester, the main character in the first book.

Today, Mr. Rockwell lives in Poughkeepsie, New York.

How to Eat Fried Worms

by Thomas Rockwell
(Dell, 1973)

(Available in Canada from Doubleday Dell Seal, in UK from Bantam Doubleday Dell, and in Australia from Transworld Publishers)

Billy, Tom, Alan, and Joe are very good friends even though they are very different. The boys have shared in many adventures together. During one friendly conversation, they discover Tom was in trouble the previous night because he would not eat his dinner. This leads to a discussion among the friends about what they would and would not eat. Billy, the daring one of the group, claims he would eat just about anything. Soon, a bet emerges. Alan bets Billy fifty dollars that Billy will not be able to eat fifteen worms in fifteen days. The boys agree to some specific rules, such as Billy will not have to eat the big green worms from tomatoes and that he can eat the worms prepared any way he wishes.

The first worm is a night crawler which has been boiled. Billy argues that it is much too large to be considered a regular worm. Tom encourages Billy to eat the first worm, enticing him with thoughts of buying a minibike with the prize money. After Billy has choked down three of the worms, Alan and Joe begin to become nervous.

By the fourth worm, Alan and Joe have come up with the first plot to try to discourage Billy from eating any other worms. When this plot fails, they come up with several other ideas to prevent Billy from winning the bet. Billy worries during this time that the worms may be making him ill, but each day he begrudgingly eats another worm.

By the tenth worm Billy's worries have been allayed. His parents have become involved in the bet and actually help him by coming up with new ways to cook worms. Billy actually begins to enjoy his daily worm meals.

Through many disagreements and physical fights, the boys' friendship endures. In the end, Billy successfully eats the fifteenth worm. Alan pays Billy the fifty dollars, and Billy agrees to share the minibike with all of his buddies. Billy finds that for some strange reason he cannot stop eating worms; he even takes a worm and egg sandwich to school for his lunch!

Vocabulary

The vocabulary words which are listed below correspond to each section of *How to Eat Fried Worms*. Ideas for vocabulary activities can be found on page 10 of this book.

SECTION 1
Chapters 1–9

squirmed	piccalilli
nagging	obsequiously
devious	fink
measly	sprawled
furtively	scrutinized
schemer	quavering
witnesses	menacingly
sly	limbering
coaxed	bleat
duel	chaff
heap	gaggles

SECTION 2
Chapters 10–15

clambered	antidote
grimacing	whimpered
keel	discernible
wailing	treacle
solemnly	deracinate
sullen	agony
hauled	wringing
suspiciously	insulting
collapsed	cringing
indignant	

SECTION 3
Chapters 16–24

triumphantly	protruding
serene	slouching
glowered	referee
glumly	neutral
offhand	dredge
disdainfully	envious
virtuous	scuttled
nonchalantly	thrashings

SECTION 4
Chapters 25–41

writhed	trembling
murmur	staggered
lunging	feebly
repetition	fulmar
incident	defrauding
clenched	stagnant
mutter	trudge
wrenched	chaffy
accusing	mussed
distressing	cistern
secrete	dejectedly

 #816 Literature Unit

Vocabulary Activity Ideas

You can help your students learn and retain the vocabulary in *How to Eat Fried Worms* by providing them with interesting vocabulary activities. Here are some ideas to try.

❑ Challenge your students to a **Vocabulary Bee!** This is similar to a spelling bee, but in addition to spelling the word correctly, the game participants must also correctly define each word.

❑ As a group activity, have your students work together to create an **Illustrated Dictionary** of the vocabulary words.

❑ Play **20 Clues** with the entire class. In this game, one student selects a vocabulary word and gives clues about this word, one by one, until someone in the class can guess the word.

❑ Ask your students to make their own **Crossword Puzzles** or **Word Search Puzzles,** using the vocabulary words from the story. Have them exchange papers and solve the puzzles. When completed, the authors can correct the papers.

❑ Have the students form a **Word Bank,** using large pieces of chart paper. Students should work together to find and define the vocabulary words from the story. Each group may be assigned specific chapters or sections of the book. When the word banks have been completed, put them in order. The class bank can be used throughout the story as a study tool to complete various activities and to prepare for the test at the end of the book.

❑ Use the words and definitions to play **Bingo.** Fold an 8½" x 11" (22 cm x 28 cm) paper into 16 squares. Have your students randomly write the words chosen for this activity in each space. The caller will read a definition, and the players will mark the correct word. Markers can be pieces of cut-up index cards, beans, or raisins. The first person to cover a row, column, or diagonal calls out, "Bingo" and is the winner. Students can swap cards and play again.

❑ Find the sentence in the book with the vocabulary word. Copy it. Rewrite the sentence by **Substituting a Synonym** which would make sense.

❑ Play **Vocabulary Charades.** In this game the words are acted out!

❑ Challenge your students to use a specific vocabulary word from the story at least **10 Times in One Day.** They must keep a record of when and how the word was used.

❑ Have the students use these words as their weekly **Spelling List.**

❑ Have the students create **Alphables** by listing the words in alphabetical order and dividing them into syllables.

❑ You probably have many more ideas to add to this list. Try them! See if experiencing vocabulary on a personal level increases your students' vocabulary interest and retention.

10

Daily Journal Activities

One way to get students involved with the reading of *How to Eat Fried Worms* is to have them keep a journal. Journal entries can be written in a special journal (see the pattern on the next page) or in a notebook. In these journals, students should be encouraged to record their thoughts based on the events of the story, make personal responses to the story, and recall event details from the story. Daily journal activities can help students organize their thoughts about the story and help them comprehend the book for later applications.

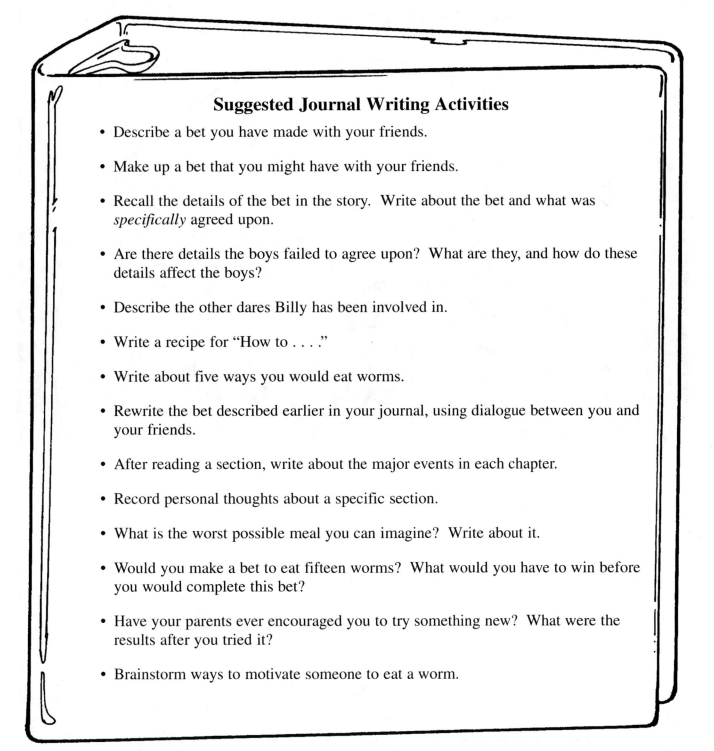

Suggested Journal Writing Activities

- Describe a bet you have made with your friends.

- Make up a bet that you might have with your friends.

- Recall the details of the bet in the story. Write about the bet and what was *specifically* agreed upon.

- Are there details the boys failed to agree upon? What are they, and how do these details affect the boys?

- Describe the other dares Billy has been involved in.

- Write a recipe for "How to . . . ."

- Write about five ways you would eat worms.

- Rewrite the bet described earlier in your journal, using dialogue between you and your friends.

- After reading a section, write about the major events in each chapter.

- Record personal thoughts about a specific section.

- What is the worst possible meal you can imagine? Write about it.

- Would you make a bet to eat fifteen worms? What would you have to win before you would complete this bet?

- Have your parents ever encouraged you to try something new? What were the results after you tried it?

- Brainstorm ways to motivate someone to eat a worm.

Daily Journal Activities *(cont.)*

Cut out the journal cover below and glue it to a folder or construction paper. Attach several sheets of writing paper to create a journal. Or, make a shape book by drawing a large worm shape and cutting it out. Then use the worm shape as a pattern to trace and cut out several pages of writing paper. Assemble the pages into a book. You will be using this journal throughout the reading of *How to Eat Fried Worms*.

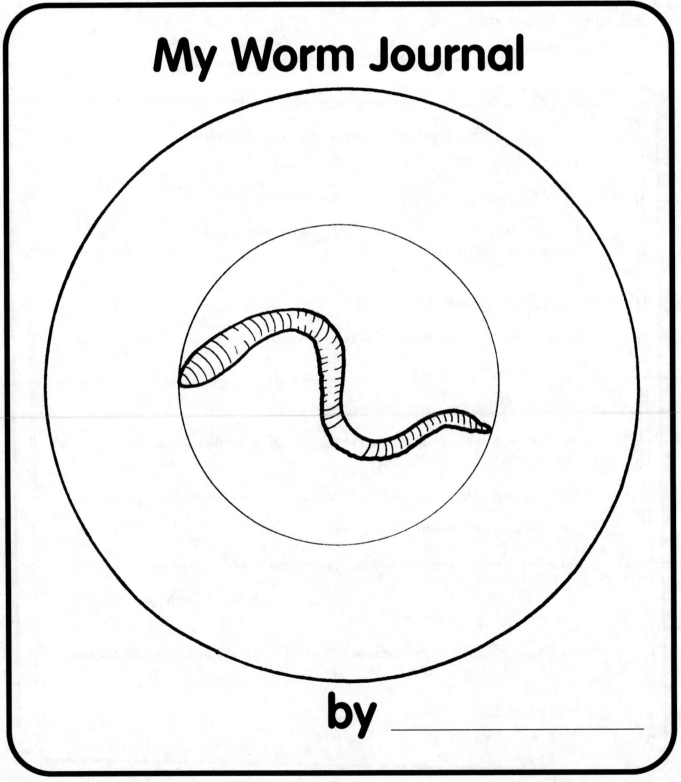

Quiz Time

1. On the back of the paper, write a one-paragraph summary of the major events in this section. Then complete the rest of the questions on this page.

2. Describe the events that lead up to the boys making the bet. What are the boys discussing?

   _____

   _____

3. What does Billy have to do to win the bet? What will he win?

   _____

   _____

4. What does Billy decide to buy with the money if he wins the bet?

   _____

5. Describe Billy's personality and the way he looks.

   _____

   _____

6. What other dares has Billy been involved in? What does this tell you about his personality?

   _____

   _____

   _____

7. Will the limbering up Billy does before eating the first worm help? Why does he do this?

   _____

   _____

8. Why does Billy get mad at the boys before he eats the first worm?

   _____

   _____

9. How does Tom help convince Billy to eat the third worm?

   _____

   _____

   _____

10. How does Billy behave after he eats the first worm? How does this behavior affect the other boys?

    _____

    _____

    _____

Character Profile

Develop one of the main characters in the story into a real person. As you fill in these blanks, try to be the character you have chosen. If you cannot answer a question with information which is given in the book, make up an answer about the character that you imagine he/she would give. When you have finished describing the character, draw a "photograph" below of how you imagine his/her appearance.

My Name _____   **Name of Character** _____

Age _____   Height _____   Weight _____   Male or Female _____

Hair Color _____   Eye Color _____   Skin Color _____

1. Where does he/she live? _____

2. Who is his/her best friend? _____

3. Describe his/her personality. _____

   _____

4. Does this character's personality remind you of yourself or anyone else you know? Who? Why? _____

   _____

5. Describe the way you imagine he/she looks. _____

   _____

6. Fill in the favorites of your character as you imagine them.

   Color _____   Food _____

   Animal _____   Hobby_____

   Sport_____   Music _____

   Place to go_____

   Thing to do _____

7. Would you like to have this character as a friend? _____

   Why or why not? _____

   _____

Poetry

In Chapter 7 Billy is reluctant to eat the third worm. He cannot stop thinking *WORM!* Tom helps him overcome his worm-track mind by encouraging him to think *FISH* instead. Tom recites a fish poem for Billy, and it seems to cheer him up. With the members of your group, write one or two verses of your own motivational worm poem. Keep in mind that you want the poem to help your friend eat a worm!

"Shark, haddock, sucker, eel,
I'll race my father in his automobile.
Eel, flounder, bluegill, shark,
We'll race all day till after dark."

_____

_____

_____

_____

_____

_____

_____

_____

_____

_____

_____

_____

Science Research Project

Steps 1 and 2

Using an encyclopedia or other nonfiction sources, find as many facts about worms as you can. Record this information below.

(The worm facts presented on page 34 may help you get started.)

_____

_____

_____

_____

_____

_____

_____

Step 2

Learn the animal classification of a worm. Find other creepy crawlies that fall into the same category. List them below. Circle the ones you would like to know more about.

_____

_____

_____

_____

_____

_____

_____

Billy and Me

Name _____

Compare yourself to Billy from the story *How to Eat Fried Worms.* Create a Venn diagram to show your similarities and differences.

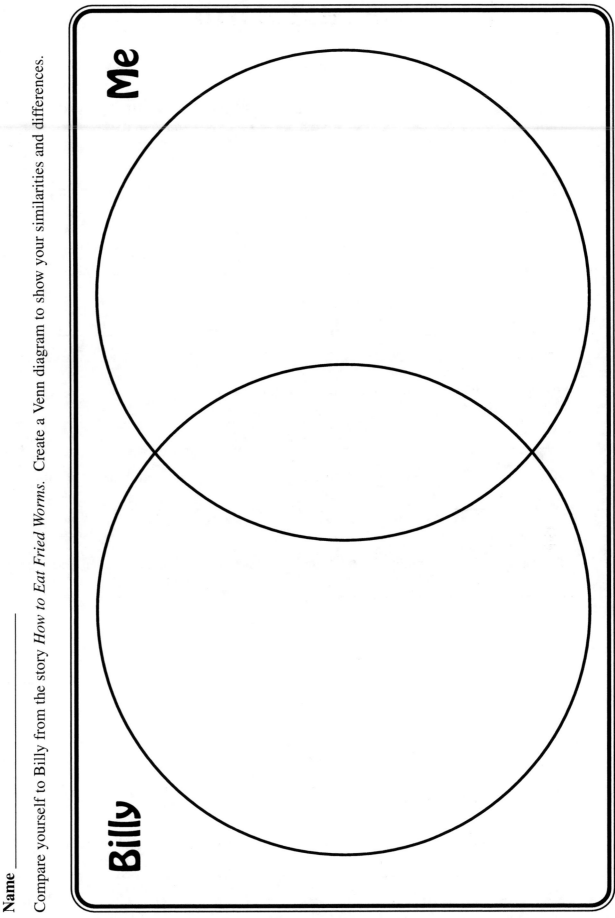

Me

Billy

Quiz Time

1. On the back of this paper, write a one-paragraph summary of the major events in this section. Then complete the rest of the questions on this page.

2. Describe the problem Alan and Joe confront Billy with in Chapter 10.

   _____

   _____

3. The problem described above leads to a big fight among the boys, even between Billy and Tom. Why do the boys fight?

   _____

   _____

4. Despite the problem, what leads Billy to eat the fifth worm?

   _____

   _____

5. Why does Alan ask his father to show him fifty dollars?

   _____

   _____

6. In Chapter 14 Billy has a dream. Describe the dream. Why do you think he has this dream?

   _____

   _____

7. After Billy awakens he realizes something he had not before. What does Billy suddenly realize?

   _____

   _____

8. Billy's realization leads to another problem. Why does Billy go into his parents' bedroom? What do his parents do?

   _____

   _____

9. What do you think is going to happen next? Why?

   _____

   _____

10. Would you continue to eat something that you thought might hurt you? Why or why not?

    _____

Worm Measurement

You will need one candy worm, a ruler, and a copy of this recording sheet.

Use your candy worm to measure the following things in the room. Record your measurements on the lines provided.

1. What is the length of the teacher's desk? _____ candy worms long

2. What is the width of the door? _____ candy worms wide

3. What is the length of the chalkboard? _____ candy worms long

4. How many worms high is your desk? _____ candy worms high

5. Choose two other things in the room to measure. Write down what you measured and their measurements.

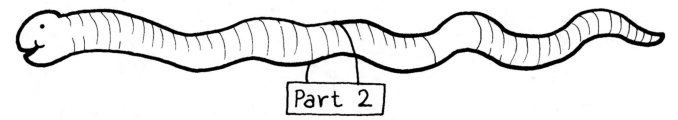

Use a standard ruler to measure how long your candy worm actually is. Record your measurement below.

My candy worm is _____ inches (_____ centimeters) long.

Compare your results with the rest of the class. You may want to record your findings on the chalkboard, making a graph to show your results.

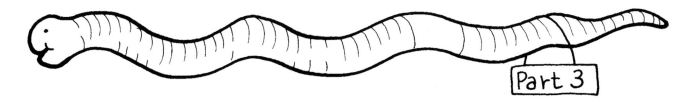

On a separate piece of paper, write any conclusions you reached about using the candy worms as a measuring tool. Consider the following questions. Would the candy worm make a good standard measuring tool? If your candy worms are the same length, did you all get the same measurements for the items in Part 1 of this activity? Is there anything you could do to the worm to make it a better measuring tool?

Worm Terrariums

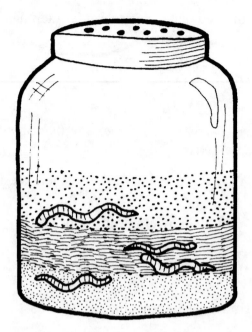

Each group will need the following materials to create a terrarium: one medium-sized jar, one plastic sandwich bag of dirt, one plastic sandwich bag of sand, black paper, and three or four earthworms.

Directions:

Layer the dirt and the sand in the jar. Be careful not to mix the dirt and the sand. Moisten the layers with a few drops of water. Add the worms to the jar and loosely cover it with the lid. Be sure that there are holes punched in the lid!

Cover the jar with black paper.

Observe the jar each day by removing the black paper only.

Moisten the soil every other day and be sure to feed your worms!

Foods Worms Love

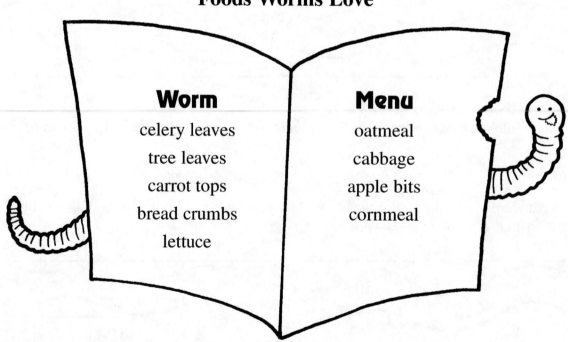

Worm

celery leaves

tree leaves

carrot tops

bread crumbs

lettuce

Menu

oatmeal

cabbage

apple bits

cornmeal

After you have made your terrarium, do the following activities in your Worm Journal.

1. Draw a picture of your terrarium after five days.

2. Draw a picture of your terrarium after ten days.

3. What conclusions can you make about worms and the effect they have on soil?

Science Research Project

Step 3

Choose one of the invertebrates from your list in Step 2 of the project. Find out as many facts as you can about your creepy crawly. Record your information below to make a fact cluster.

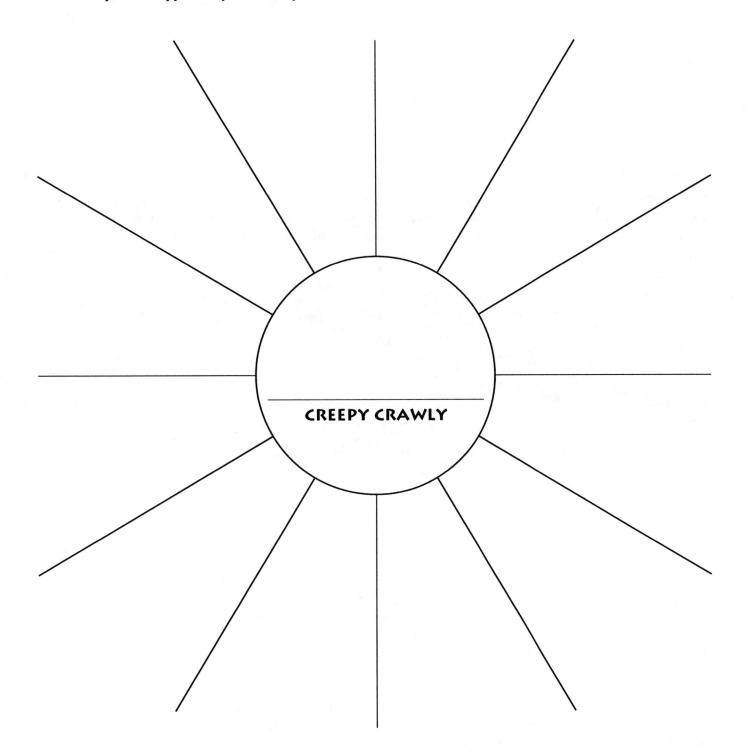

CREEPY CRAWLY

Sentence Strips

Even after reading a book chapter by chapter very carefully, you may find you still have some questions about the story. You may need clarification as to what event happened to which character, what the character looks like, where the story takes place, or how the events of the story lead to one another. To help clarify who, what, when, where, or how in the story *How to Eat Fried Worms,* do the following activity.

Materials:

- sentence strips or strips of paper
- pencil or marker
- clay (molded to form "question mark" shaped worms)
- elbow pasta
- small, round candies
- glue

Directions:

Brainstorm any questions you may have about *How to Eat Fried Worms* in your Worm Journal. Choose up to three to write on three different sentence strips. Use the clay worm to make the question mark at the end of the sentence. When necessary, use the elbow noodles for quotation marks or commas and the candies for periods in your sentences.

Did Billy really feel sick from the worms ?

Tom said, "Boiled, stewed, fried, fricasseed." What does "fricasseed" mean ?

What was Billy worried about in Chapter 15 ?

Teacher Tip:

You may want to display these questions on the chalkboard or bulletin board and then hold a class question-and-answer period. Allow your students to read their sentence strip questions and then ask their classmates for answers. This will help with the overall comprehension of the story and assist students in preparing for the chapter and final tests.

Quiz Time

1. On the back of this paper, write a one-paragraph summary of the major events in this section. Then complete the rest of the questions on this page.

2. What did Billy know that helped him gulp the worm "triumphantly, serene, untroubled?"

   _____

   _____

3. Why does Billy seem to ignore Tom when he returns to witness the eighth worm?

   _____

   _____

4. Explain Alan and Joe's second scheme they use in an attempt to prevent Billy from winning the bet. (Chapter 19)

   _____

   _____

5. What causes Billy to become suspicious of the ninth worm?

   _____

   _____

6. Alan and Joe pay Billy's mom a visit. What happens when they fink on Billy and tell her what he has been eating?

   _____

   _____

7. What do Alan and Joe ask Billy's mom to do for them? Explain Mrs. Forrester's attitude towards the bet and what she has to do. How does she help with the bet?

   _____

   _____

   _____

8. Describe the next scheme Alan and Joe come up with to try to trick Billy into losing the bet.

   _____

   _____

9. The boys are having a hard time agreeing on the terms of the bet, and as a result they argue. What could the boys have done early on to prevent these disagreements?

   _____

   _____

10. If you were to make a similar bet, what rules would you suggest?

   _____

   _____

Literal and Figurative Statements

Throughout the book there are several plays on words or *figurative* statements which are not to be taken literally. Look up the words *literal* and *figurative* in the dictionary. Write the definitions below.

Literal _____

Figurative _____

Now think of five figurative statements. An example of a figurative statement is, "Put a sock in it!" The literal meaning would be to put a sock into your mouth. The figurative meaning would be to tell someone to stop talking.

1. _____

2. _____

3. _____

4. _____

5. _____

The following are examples of figurative statements from the book. On the lines provided, write the literal meaning and the figurative meaning of each statement.

1. Billy said Joe and Alan "couldn't lick a flea."

   Literal _____

   Figurative _____

2. Alan said Billy was "chicken."

   Literal _____

   Figurative _____

3. Tom wanted to "make a break for it."

   Literal _____

   Figurative _____

4. Billy said Joe and Alan were "weaseling."

   Literal _____

   Figurative _____

5. Billy said that the night crawler was "as big as a souvenir pencil."

   Literal _____

   Figurative _____

6. **Challenge:** See if you can find any other figurative statements in the story and write them on the back of this page.

Worm Report

Worms fall into a special category of animals called invertebrates. Invertebrates are animals without backbones. Using a real worm, conduct the following experiments.

Locate the following parts of the worm. As you find the part on your worm, draw a picture of it in the space below. Be sure to label each part. Color your drawing the same color as your worm.

Be careful! Some parts listed below cannot be found on a worm! You may want to use an encyclopedia to help you.

Eyes	Legs	Tail	Bristles
Mouth	Head	Segments or Rings	Clitellum

Conduct the following extra experiments with your worm.

1. Place the worm on a piece of clear plastic or glass. Can you see through the worm's body? Can you see its blood vessels or its beating heart?

2. Turn the worm onto its back. Watch how it flips itself over.

3. Place the worm on a damp paper towel. Find the pairs of small bristles and gently touch them. What do they feel like?

4. Write several sentences summarizing your experiences with the worm.

Science Research Project

Steps 4 and 5

Step 4

Using the information you have obtained from Steps 1–3 design a project to show your results. You may want to brainstorm some project ideas in the space below. When you have decided on a project, talk it over with your teacher and then begin!

Project Suggestions:

- Newspaper Report—Report your information as a newscaster.
- Activity—Present an overview of your findings and then make up a crossword puzzle for your classmates to work on when you are finished with your presentation.
- Dress Up—Dress as your creepy crawly and give a report.
- Collage—Make a large creepy crawly display illustrating your findings.
- Crawly Sharing—Bring the creepy crawly you researched to school and share your findings with the class.

These are just a few ideas; now brainstorm to come up with other ideas. Unique ideas are always welcome!

Brainstorm

Step 5

On a separate piece of paper, plan your project. Include the answers to the questions below.

A. How am I going to present the information? What type of project am I going to do?

B. What information do I need to include?

C. What materials do I need to get started on my project?

Once your outline is complete and you have answered the questions, begin making your research project.

Wormy Recipes

Chocolate Covered Worms

Ingredients:

- 1 or 2 packages of candy worms

- 1 package (12 oz.) semisweet chocolate morsels

- 2–3 tablespoons (30–45mL) shortening

Melt the chocolate chips in a saucepan. Add 2–3 tablespoons of shortening to the chocolate to give it a smooth and shiny consistency. Hold the end of the worm with tongs and dip the worm into the chocolate. Remove the worm from the chocolate and place it on a piece of waxed paper. Allow the worms to cool and harden for 20–30 minutes. The worms can be placed in the refrigerator to speed up the cooling process. When the chocolate is set, the worms will loosen from the waxed paper. You are now ready to enjoy "Vurm à la Chocolate!"

Mud

Ingredients:

- 1 (5.9 oz. or 167.2 g.) package instant chocolate pudding

- 1 tub of frozen whipped topping, thawed

- 1 package chocolate sandwich cookies, crushed

- 1 package candy worms

Make the chocolate pudding according to the package directions. Fold the whipped topping into the pudding. Using a clear plastic cup, layer the pudding and the crushed cookies up to about 1 inch (2.5 cm) from the top. Arrange 3–4 candy worms along the top so that they look as though they are coming out of the mud. You are now ready to enjoy some delicious worm-infested mud!

Quiz Time

1. On the back of this paper, write a one-paragraph summary of the major events that happen in this section. Then complete the rest of the questions on this page.

2. Alan and Joe are very excited because they think they have won the bet. Describe in detail the events that take place next.

   _____

   _____

   _____

3. What is Mr. Phelps' reaction when he finds out what Alan has done to Billy?

   _____

4. What does Alan's father make the boys do as punishment?

   _____

   _____

5. What happens to cause the "Peace Treaty" discussion with the boys' fathers? What is the result of that discussion?

   _____

   _____

6. Billy thinks he has won the bet after he eats the fifteenth worm. What happens to Billy to make him realize something is very wrong? What had Alan and Joe done?

   _____

   _____

7. Why does Alan charge Billy just before he eats the fifteenth worm? What do Alan and Joe do with Billy?

   _____

   _____

8. What event occurs to prevent Billy from eating the final worm?

   _____

   _____

9. Describe how Billy gets the final worm.

   _____

   _____

10. What unexpected event occurs in the final chapter?

   _____

   _____

Playing Tricks

Below is a list of tricky words. These words all involve a scheme or plot that Alan and Joe come up with to try to trick Billy. Write a summary highlighting the details of each trick and why each trick is ultimately unsuccessful.

1. glue _____

   _____

   _____

2. Shea Stadium _____

   _____

   _____

3. doctor's letter _____

   _____

   _____

4. kidney beans _____

   _____

   _____

5. cistern _____

   _____

   _____

6. the 4th worm _____

   _____

   _____

Create a Game

The rules and details of the bet among the characters in the story were not clearly laid out. In several instances the lack of details was the reason the boys argued. To practice creating rules, make up a new game with the members of your group.

Before designing your game, organize your general ideas about it by filling in the blanks below.

Name of the Game _____

Purpose of the Game _____

Number of Players _____

Special Information About the Game _____

_____

_____

Materials/Equipment _____

_____

Determining the Winner (How Do You Win the Game?)_____

_____

_____

Make a game board, using a large sheet of construction or chart paper. Remember that the game should be colorful and bright, just like commercially-made games, so that it will attract players. Once you have completed your game, have a trial run, playing the game with your group members in order to work out any of the problems you may have. Write the directions and rules to your game on the following page. Attach this rule sheet to the back of your game so that others playing the game will have easy access to the rules. When your game has been completed to the group's satisfaction switch, games with another group. Were the directions to other games easy to follow? Did any arguments/disagreements erupt?

Teacher's Note: You may want to have a game day prior to the start of this activity. Students may bring in commercially-made games from home and share them with the class. Allow the groups to rotate through the games so that the students get the opportunity to play more than one game.

Create a Game *(cont.)*

Directions:

First, _____

_____

_____

Next, _____

_____

_____

Then, _____

_____

_____

Last, _____

_____

_____

Rules: _____

_____

_____

_____

_____

_____

Science Research Project

Steps 6 and 7

Step 6

Practice presenting your project with a partner. Ask your partner to honestly critique your presentation, considering such things as eye contact, volume, length of the presentation, and the information given. Your partner may write suggestions and positive remarks on the lines below.

_____

_____

_____

_____

Step 7

Use the following request form to indicate the day that you would like to present your project to the class. Cut out the form and give it to your teacher, and he/she will return it, confirming your presentation day and time. Good luck and have fun!

_____

_____

_____

_____

Name _____

Presentation Topic _____

Requested Date of Presentation _____

Assigned Presentation Date and Time

_____

Worm du Jour

In the book *How to Eat Fried Worms*, Billy enjoys worms in a variety of ways. Every day he eats one boiled, à la mode, fried, or raw. Billy's mother even helps with the bet by looking for new ways to cook the worms for Billy. In the space provided, write a new recipe for "worm." Use the back of this paper, if neccessary. Share your recipe with the rest of the class.

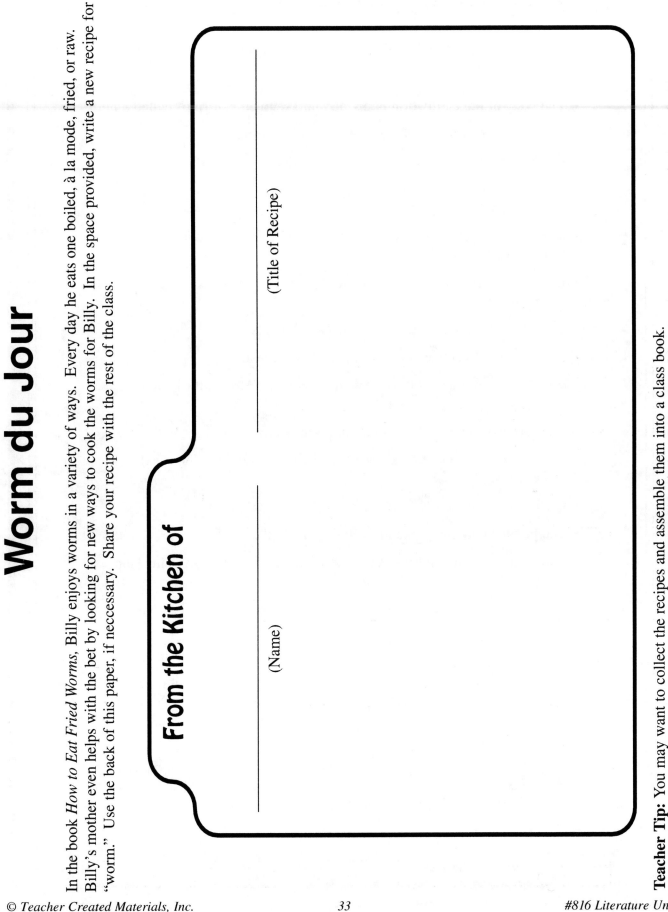

From the Kitchen of

_____
(Name)

_____
(Title of Recipe)

Teacher Tip: You may want to collect the recipes and assemble them into a class book.

Worm Facts

- The body of the earthworm is divided into segments or rings called *annuli*.

- Earthworms can be as short as $\frac{1}{25}$ of an inch (.1 cm).

- Earthworms can be as long as 3 feet (91 cm).

- Earthworms do not have eyes. Each segment of an earthworm has a pair of spots which detect light.

- An earthworm is moist to the touch because of a slimy coating which keeps it from drying out.

- If an earthworm's head or tail is cut off, it will grow back. This is called *regeneration*.

- Earthworms eat leaves, grass, and decayed plants.

- Earthworms are active at night; this is when they eat.

- There are more than 3,000 species of earthworms found throughout the world.

- The earthworm's mouth is on the first segment.

- An earthworm has bristles on the underside of its body. The bristles help it move through the soil.

- Earthworms can be red, grey, or brown.

- The pointed end that looks like a tail is really the head.

- Earthworms are helpful in keeping the soil rich in nutrients. This helps plants to grow.

- The earthworm makes tunnels in the dirt as it moves. This loosens the soil, allowing water and air to circulate and helping plants to grow.

- The earthworm does have keen senses of touch, smell, and taste.

- An earthworm does not have lungs. The worm gets oxygen through its skin. The earthworm must remain moist, but it cannot tolerate too much water or it might drown. The worm comes to the surface during heavy rains to avoid drowning.

- The worm moves by contracting its circular and long muscles that run throughout its body. The forward part of the worm's body has five pairs of hearts. Blood is pumped by muscular action.

Any Questions?

When you finished reading *How to Eat Fried Worms,* did you have some questions that were left unanswered? Write your questions here.

_____

_____

_____

_____

_____

Work in groups or by yourself to prepare some possible answers for the questions you asked above and those written below. When you have finished, hold a class forum to share your ideas with the rest of the group.

- Why are the chapters named as they are?

- How do the titles reflect what the chapters are about?

- Are the boys really best friends? Why or why not?

- Why did Alan and Joe try to trick Billy?

- What problems does the bet cause among the boys?

- How are these problems resolved in the end?

- How does Tom help, or not help, Billy throughout the story?

- Describe Tom's personality.

- Do Billy's parents react in a predictable way?

- What do Billy's parents do throughout the bet?

- Is it unusual that Billy would be involved in such a bet? Why or why not?

- Would Tom ever involve himself in such a bet? Why or why not?

- What could the boys have done very early on to avoid some of the problems they had?

- What are the conditions of the bet?

- Who are the unlikely heroes at the end of the story?

- Are these characters critical to Billy's winning of the bet?

- Do the boys remain friends at the end of the story? How do you know?

- What do you think happened to Alan? Was he punished?

- What unexpected event occurs in the Epilogue?

Book Report Ideas

There are numerous ways to report on a book once you have read it. After you have finished reading *How to Eat Fried Worms,* choose one method of reporting that interests you. It may be a way your teacher suggests, an idea of your own, or one of the ways that is mentioned below.

- **See What I Read?**

  This report is a visual one. A model of a favorite scene and characters can be created, using a shoe box as a diorama or a drawing of the scene on paper.

- **Book Reviewer**

  Pretend to be a book reviewer and give all of the important information about the book. Give just enough information to entice the audience and then close the report just before divulging how the story ends.

- **The Sequel**

  Write a part two for the story, predicting what might happen if the story were to continue.

- **Lights! Camera! Action!**

  In a small group, prepare a scene from the story for dramatization. Act it out and relate the significance of the scene to the entire book. Add costumes and props to set the stage.

- **Ad Piece**

  Design an advertising piece for the book. Choose an audience to target in order to encourage them to read the book. Include some kind of graphics or visual aid in your presentation.

- **Dress Up**

  Design a costume for a favorite character from the book. Wear the costume during the report. Talk as though you are the character. Include important information from the book as it relates to the character.

- **Literary Interview**

  This report is done in pairs. One student will pretend to be a character in the story. The other student will play the role of a television or radio interviewer, providing the audience with insights into the character's personality and life. It is the responsibility of the partners to create meaningful questions and appropriate responses.

Crossword Puzzle

Use the clues on page 38 to fill in the puzzle grid.

Crossword Puzzle *(cont.)*

Use these clues to fill in the grid on the previous page. The answers to the clues are all listed in the vocabulary box.

Across

1. Good, righteous
4. Charging with a fault or crime
9. A gull-like bird
10. Bending the body easily; flexing
12. To shake or quiver
13. Crying a long, high-pitched sound in grief or suffering
15. An informer or spy
18. To mock or tease, or the husks of grasses
19. To pull up by the roots
20. To utter words in a low tone
21. A remedy, cure

Down

2. Talked into something
3. To walk or stand unsteadily
5. A tank for storing water
6. Gloomy and silent
7. Making a facial expression of pain or disapproval
8. Pulled with force or carried away
11. Flocks of geese
14. Jealous
15. Sly, shifty, underhanded
16. Combat between two people
17. Unconcernedly, coolly
22. To dig up

Vocabulary Box

coaxed	dredge	virtuous	accusing
fink	wailing	nonchalantly	fulmar
duel	deracinate	envious	cistern
chaff	sullen	mutter	
furtive	antidote	stagger	

"How to . . ." Speech

──── Organization ────

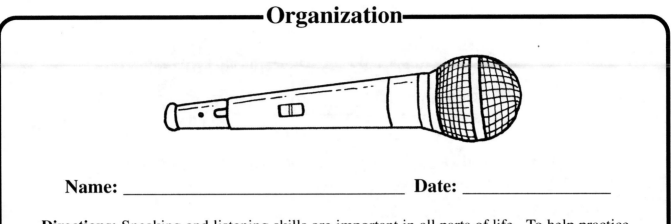

Name: _____ **Date:** _____

Directions: Speaking and listening skills are important in all parts of life. To help practice these skills, you will be developing a "How to . . . ." speech. During your "How to . . ." speech, you will be teaching us how to do something. For instance, you may choose to teach us how to tie shoelaces, brush teeth, or make a peanut butter and jelly sandwich. Pick a topic that interests you and remember to include details and props!

Brainstorm: Alone or with a partner, brainstorm a list of possible "How to . . ." topics. Write your ideas in the box below.

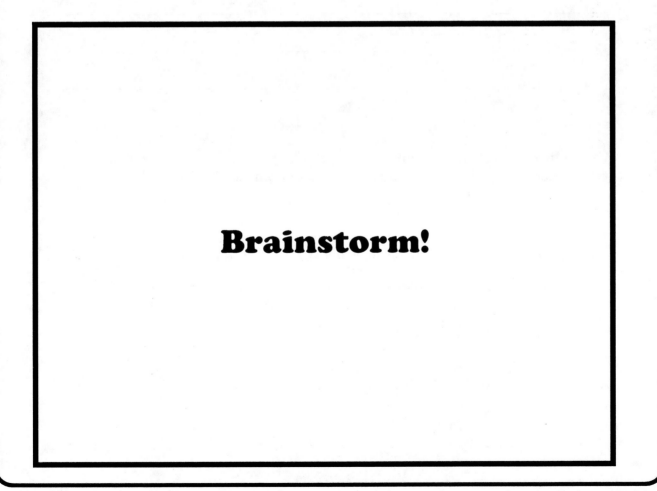

Brainstorm!

"How to . . ." Speech (cont.)

Planning

Select a Topic: Choose a topic from your brainstormed list (on the previous page) for your "How to . . ." speech.

My Topic: _____

Props: Make a list of props needed for your speech. Also include how and where you will get the props.

_____

_____

_____

_____

_____

Group Involvement: Decide how you are going to get your audience involved in your speech. (This will help ensure that you have been an effective teacher!)

Some ideas include . . .

> . . . a crossword puzzle. Make up a puzzle which uses key words for answers. Ask your classmates to complete the puzzle after your speech.

> . . . a test. After giving your speech, ask your classmates general questions about your presentation.

> . . . a demonstration. Challenge your audience to actually demonstrate what you have taught them.

Brainstorm other possible involvement ideas on the back of this paper. Circle the one you will use.

"How to . . ." Speech *(cont.)*

─Preparation─

Outlining the Speech: Put the steps of your speech in order. Assume that your audience does not know how to do what you are going to show them. Write your steps on the lines below. Number the steps. Be very specific and clear, and be sure to include all of the steps in a logical order. Use only as many blanks as you need.

_____

_____

_____

_____

_____

_____

_____

_____

Practice: Prior to giving your speech to your classmates, practice giving the speech to two different people (separately) at home. Make any necessary changes/adjustments to your speech.

Who are the two people who helped you practice? Ask them to sign their names below and write any suggestions they might have.

1. _____

Suggestions: _____

_____

2. _____

Suggestions: _____

_____

"How to . . ." Speech (cont.)

Presentation

Presentation Day: Ask yourself the following questions:

- Do I have all of the necessary props?

- Have I included a group involvement activity?

- Does my speech follow a logical sequence?

Finally, while delivering your speech, remember to relax, enjoy yourself, and have fun!

Evaluation: Evaluate how well you think you delivered your speech. Was your goal met? Did the audience learn how to do what you demonstrated?

_____

_____

Write a paragraph summary of your presentation in the space below. You may use the book, if necessary.

_____

_____

_____

_____

_____

_____

_____

_____

Unit Test

Matching: Match the quote with the person who said it. Write the speakers' names in the correct blanks.

Billy   Mrs. Forrester   Joe   Pete   Mr. O'Hara
Tom   Alan   Mr. Forrester   Mr. Phelps

1. _____ "There will be no repetition of this incident or anything like it."

2. _____ "I just said if the first four worms didn't kill you, this one wouldn't."

3. _____ "They're big worms, Mrs. Forrester." "We won't lie to you. My mother told me never to tell a lie."

4. _____ "Catch!"

5. _____ "That's stupid, one bite can't hurt you. I'd eat one bite of anything before I'd let them send me up to my room right after supper."

6. _____ "All right. And thirdly, I ate a live crayfish when I was in college and have suffered no discernible ill effects. And fourthly: I am going to sleep."

7. _____ "You four boys have been friends too long to start fighting now."

8. _____ "Yeah, well—oh geez, how'd I ever get into this? If my father finds out—"

9. _____ "Well, this is quite a responsibility. Are you sure I'll be neutral enough?"

True or False: Write true or false next to each statement.

1. _____ Tom encourages Billy to eat a worm by singing a song.

2. _____ Poison control tells Billy's dad that eating worms can be harmful.

3. _____ Alan and Joe plot against Billy by taking him to the baseball game.

4. _____ Mrs. Forrester is furious and refuses to feed worms to Billy.

5. _____ Billy never has a problem eating the worms.

Short Answer: On a separate piece of paper, provide a short answer for each of these questions. Be sure to clearly number each of your answers.

1. Why do Billy's parents call poison control?

2. Who saves Billy from losing the bet at the end of the book?

3. What does Billy discover when he burps after the first fifteenth worm?

4. How does Billy react after eating the first couple of worms?

5. Why is Alan so nervous about the bet?

Essay: Answer these questions on a separate piece of paper.

1. Describe the personalities of the four boys, Alan, Billy, Joe, and Tom. Are they alike or different? What helps them to be and stay close friends?

2. How do Alan and Joe try to trick Billy? Describe in detail two of the plots.

Response

Directions: Explain the meaning of each of these quotations from *How to Eat Fried Worms.*

Chapter 1   *Yeah, but we provide the worms. And there have to be witnesses present when he eats them; either me or Alan or somebody we can trust. Not just you and Billy.*

Chapter 2   *There's nothing wrong with manure. It comes from cows, just like milk.*

Chapter 4   *Did you see their* faces*? Climbing over each other out the door? Oh! Geez! Joe was pale as an onion.*

Chapter 5   *If he doesn't give up himself, I'll figure something out. We could spike the next worm with pepper.*

Chapter 6   *But it makes me feel sort of sick. Even* before *I eat it. Just thinking about it.*

Chapter 7   *I'll put parsley around it, and some slices of lemon. And then you can concentrate, think fish. All the time you're waiting in the barn, all the time you're eating it, keep saying to yourself: fish fish fish . . . .*

Chapter 9   *Geez, you think it'll work? Suppose it doesn't? He didn't seem to pay much attention today.*

Chapter 10   *It's just something Joe's father told him the other night. It's nothing.*

Chapter 11   *Then I'll go dig* another *worm, just for him. He's so* big*, telling me; 'Hurry up, hurry up, I can't wait around all day—don't be a sissy.'*

Chapter 15   *One this afternoon. I've eaten one every day for the last five days. But they weren't little ones; they were night crawlers, huge ones, as big as snakes almost.*

Chapter 19   *That's not a* worm! *How can it be a worm? Geez, it must be* two feet long!

Chapter 20   *I don't know if you know about it already, but see, about a week ago Alan made this bet with Billy about eating worms.*

Chapter 21   *We'll all* have *worm tonight.*

Chapter 23   *Look, even if he remembers the worm while we're at Shea, he can't get one. Where's anyone going to find a worm at Shea Stadium?*

Chapter 29   *So what? We can lick both of you with our hands tied behind our backs and paper bags over our heads.*

Teacher Note: Choose an appropriate number of quotes for your students.

Conversations

Work in groups to write and perform the conversations that might have occurred in each of the following situations.

* ✱ Alan, Tom, and Billy discuss where Tom was the previous night. (3 people)

* ✱ The boys disagree on where to dig for the worms. (3 people)

* ✱ Billy recalls with a friend how people are always daring him to do things. (2 people)

* ✱ Tom encourages Billy to continue eating the worms by talking about the fun they will have on the minibike. (2 people)

* ✱ The boys have a conversation before, during, and after the first worm. (3 or 4 people)

* ✱ Tom and Billy have a fight about eating the worms. (2 people)

* ✱ Alan and Joe are convinced Billy is going to quit by the fifth worm. (2 people)

* ✱ Alan is very worried about losing the bet and telephones Joe late at night. (2 people)

* ✱ Billy enters his parents' bedroom at 3:15 a.m. (3 people)

* ✱ The ninth worm causes some problems among the boys. (3 people)

* ✱ Alan and Joe confront Billy's mom with the news; Billy is still eating worms. (3 people)

* ✱ Mrs. Forrester agrees to feed Billy worms while Alan and Joe are gone. (2 people)

* ✱ Alan and Joe have to go around the neighborhood apologizing. (several people)

* ✱ Alan and Joe lock Billy in the cistern. (3 people)

Perform one of your own conversation ideas for the characters in *How to Eat Fried Worms*. Write your conversation idea on the lines below.

_____

_____

_____

_____

_____

_____

Bibliography

Related Stories

Ahlberg, Janet and Allan. *The Little Worm Book.* (Viking Press, 1980)

Rippon, Sally. *Willy Worm.* (Rourke Corp., 1982)

Robinson, Barbara. *My Brother Louis Measures Worms and Other Louis Stories.* (Harper and Row, 1988)

Rockwell, Thomas. *How to Eat Fried Worms and Other Plays.* (Delacorte Press, 1980)

Stapp, Arthur. *The Fabulous Earthworm Deal.* (Viking Press, 1969)

Thomas, Ruth. *Worms Wiggle, Bugs Jiggle.* (Reader's Digest, 1982)

Nonfiction

Coldrey, Jennifer. *Discovering Worms.* (Watts,1986)

Darling, Lois and Louis. *Worms.* (Morrow, 1972)

Johnson, Sylvia, A. *Silkworms.* (Lerner, 1982)

Kallen, Stuart. *If Animals Could Talk.* (Rockbottom Books, 1993)

Kalman, Bobbie and Janine Schaub. *Squirmy Wormy Composters.* (Charlotte Publisher, 1992)

McLaughlin, Molly. *Earthworms, Dirt, and Rotten Leaves: An Exploration in Ecology*. (Macmillan, 1986)

Nichols, David. *Oxford Book of Invertebrates.* (Oxford University Press, 1971)

Simon and Seymour. *Pets in a Jar: Collecting and Caring for Small Wild Animals.* (Viking Press, 1975)

Other Books by Thomas Rockwell

How to Fight a Girl (Dell, 1988)

How to Get Fabulously Rich (Watts, 1990)

Answer Key

Page 13

1. Accept appropriate responses.
2. The boys are discussing why Tom did not meet with the others the night before. He was punished because he would not eat salmon casserole. This leads to the boys discussing that one bite of anything cannot hurt you, including a worm.
3. Alan bets Billy fifty dollars that he cannot eat one worm each day for fifteen days.
4. minibike
5. He is chunky with freckles and snub nose. He is very daring and courageous in that he is always accepting challenges that other people dare him to do.
6. Billy was dared to sleep outside in an igloo that he and the boys had made. He was also dared to put on all of his winter clothes when it was ninety-five degrees outside and walk up and down main street.
7. Accept appropriate responses.
8. Billy gets angry because the worm is so big.
9. Tom sings a song about fish and minibikes.
10. Billy acts a little crazy. This scares the other boys.

Page 18

1. Accept appropriate responses.
2. Alan and Joe try to convince Billy that eating worms can be unhealthy.
3. Billy isn't sure what to think about the tale Alan and Joe tell. Billy gets angry with Tom because Tom is so nonchalant, and he is not the one eating the worms.
4. Billy does not want to lose. Alan and Joe think he is going to quit.
5. Alan is getting nervous that he will lose the bet. He wants to see just how much fifty dollars is.
6. Accept appropriate responses.
7. Billy realizes that maybe Alan and Joe were telling the truth, that worms really are harmful if eaten.
8. Billy has terrible pain in his stomach. He goes to his parents to tell them what he has been eating. His father calls poison control and finds out that there are no ill effects from eating worms.
9. Accept appropriate responses.

10. Accept appropriate responses.

Page 23

1. Accept appropriate responses.
2. Billy knows that eating a worm will not hurt him. He has confidence.
3. Billy is still irritated with Tom because he deserted him earlier.
4. Alan and Joe glue two worms together.
5. It is so long. He scrapes the cornmeal off to find the glue.
6. Billy's mom is upset that he is still eating worms but knows that they cannot harm him.
7. The boys ask Mrs. Forrester to feed the worms to Billy while they are gone on a trip. She seems ready to help them out, and she looks for some new recipes. She cooks some unique recipes for worms for Billy.
8. Alan and Joe decide to take Billy to a baseball game and feed him all kinds of junk food, hoping he will be too stuffed and tired to remember the worm.
9. Accept appropriate responses.
10. Accept appropriate responses.

Page 28

1. Accept appropriate responses.
2. Billy remembers he hasn't eaten a worm. They find a worm, awaken the neighborhood, and Billy eats the 13th worm.
3. He is upset with Alan and speaks to him sternly.
4. As a punishment they must knock on all the neighbors' doors and apologize.
5. The boys get into a bad physical fight and are scratched and bruised as a result. The boys agree to make up to get ice cream.
6. He burps up beans, not worm. Alan and Joe had made the worm out of beans.
7. Alan is desperate to prevent Billy from winning the bet. In a last effort he tackles him, and they throw him into the cistern.
8. Billy is locked in the cistern. His dad discovers him and sends him to his room with no questions or discussion about it. Mr. Forrester has had it.
9. Pete, Tom's younger brother, brings the worm in a basket and throws it up into Billy's opened window.
10. Billy eats worms all the time and loves them.

Answer Key *(cont.)*

Page 29

1. glue—Alan and Joe glue two worms together to try to trick Billy.
2. Shea Stadium—Alan and Joe take Billy to a baseball game, feed him junk food, and bring him home late, hoping he will forget to eat a worm.
3. doctor's letter—Alan and Joe write a letter, pretending to be a doctor and explaining that worms are very bad for your health and should not be eaten.
4. kidney beans—The first fifteenth worm is really made out of kidney beans.
5. cistern—It is the hole Alan and Joe put Billy in to prevent him from eating another worm.
6. the 4th worm—Joe tries to tell Billy that his family is furious that he might be eating worms because they are very unhealthy.

Page 37

Across
1. virtuous
4. accusing
9. fulmar
10. limbering
12. quaver
13. wailing
15. fink
18. chaff
19. deracinate
20. mutter
21. antidote

Down
2. coaxed
3. stagger
5. cistern
6. sullen
7. grimacing
8. hauled
11. gaggles
14. envious
15. furtive
16. duel
17. nonchalantly

22. dredge

Page 43

Matching
1. Mr. Phelps
2. Tom
3. Joe
4. Pete
5. Billy
6. Mr. Forrester
7. Mr. O'Hara
8. Alan
9. Mrs. Forrester

True or False
1. True
2. False
3. True
4. False
5. False

Short Answer
1. They are worried that eating worms may be dangerous to Billy's health.
2. Tom's brother Pete brings the fifteenth worm to Billy.
3. Billy burps up beans.
4. Billy acts as though he is going crazy to scare the others. He also cannot stop thinking "worm," and it makes him feel sick.
5. He is worried about where he is going to get the money and what his parents are going to do and say to him.

Essay
1. Accept appropriate responses.
2. Accept appropriate responses.

Page 44

Accept all reasonable responses.

Page 45

Perform the conversations (dramas) in class. Ask the students to respond to the conversations in several different ways, such as, "Are the conversations realistic?" or "Are the words the characters saying in keeping with their personalities?"